Puma cub

Porcupette

Hamster pup

ANIMAL PLANET

ANIMAL BITES

baby animals

Dorothea DePrisco

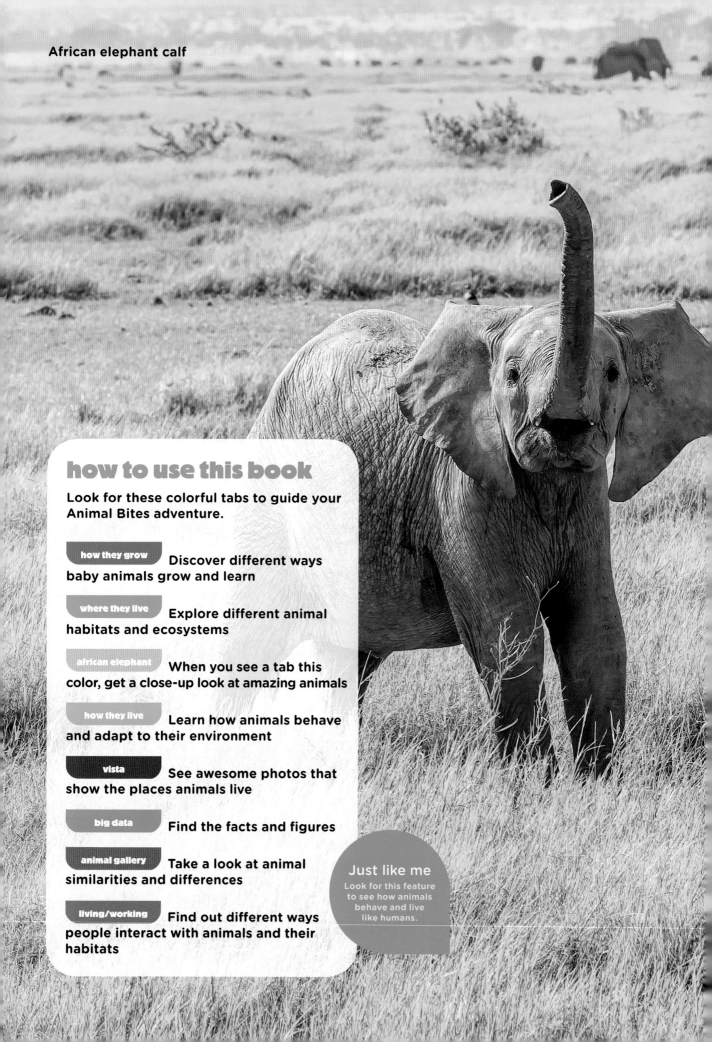

African elephant calf

how to use this book

Look for these colorful tabs to guide your Animal Bites adventure.

how they grow Discover different ways baby animals grow and learn

where they live Explore different animal habitats and ecosystems

african elephant When you see a tab this color, get a close-up look at amazing animals

how they live Learn how animals behave and adapt to their environment

vista See awesome photos that show the places animals live

big data Find the facts and figures

animal gallery Take a look at animal similarities and differences

living/working Find out different ways people interact with animals and their habitats

Just like me
Look for this feature to see how animals behave and live like humans.

table of contents

how they grow
Breaking out 6

spotted owlet
Owl be seeing you 8

where they live
Not just for the birds 10

how they grow
Born ready 12

red panda
One of a kind 14

vista
Mother knows best 16

how they grow
Baby time 18

saint bernard dog
Dog-gone it 20

living
The buddy system 22

animal gallery
Handful of cute 24

spotted eagle ray
On the spot 26

vista
It's a croc! 28

how they live
Baby on board 30

angora rabbit
A honey of a bunny 32

how they grow
Dinner's ready 34

where they live
Peek-a-boo 36

how they live
Love shows the way 38

flatid planthopper
Bedazzle this! 40

vista
Going my way? 42

how they grow
Making changes 44

striped skunk
Scent-sational! 46

animal gallery
Egg-cellent 48

big data
The stackup 50

how they live
The sister and brother act 52

maine coon cat
Claw-some cutie 54

animal gallery
Solos and siblings 56

how they grow
Mini me 58

where they live
Hiding out 60

northern raccoon
A masked bandit 62

working
Turning things around 64

vista
Special tail-ent 66

how they live
Family ties 68

sea otter
Otter-ly adorable 70

big data
Habitat habits 72

Activities and resources 74

Glossary 76

Index 78

Photo credits 80

Breaking out

Many animals lay eggs. As the babies develop, they are protected by hard-shelled eggs, egg cases, and cocoons. When they're ready, they break out and begin their lives.

Coral reef spawning

Some coral reefs reproduce through a process called mass spawning. They release huge clouds of male and female cells that form offspring. They settle on the ocean floor and form new coral.

That's amazing

Nearly all mammals give birth to live young. But the duck-billed platypus lays eggs! After ten days, the eggs hatch. The babies nurse (drink their mother's milk) for about four months.

Big family

A praying mantis can lay about 250 eggs in one small sac. It is soft at first, then hardens to protect the eggs. Nymphs emerge from the sac. They continue to grow until they are adults. This three-step process is called simple metamorphosis.

1 Egg

4 Monarch Butterfly

A real beauty!

A butterfly starts out as a tiny egg. It goes through four stages as it grows into a beautiful butterfly. This is called complete metamorphosis.

2 Larva (Caterpillar)

3 Chrysalis (Pupa)

Owl be seeing you

This baby was born with its eyes closed. At one to two weeks old, its eyes will open. At six weeks, the chick will be able to fly. It will take six months for all of its adult feathers to grow in.

Soft **white down** covers the baby owlet's **pink skin.**

The **beak** has a bump on top called an egg tooth that is used to break out of its shell. This is called "pipping."

Once the **wing feathers** grow in, the owlet can begin to hop and fly. This takes about a month.

PET-WORTHY?

☐ YES ☒ NO

It looks adorable, but this baby is a fierce hunter in the making, with a sharp beak and razorlike talons.

INFO BITES

Name: Spotted Owlet

Type of animal: Bird

Home: Open country in Southern Asia

Baby fact: Once a chick grows wing feathers and is strong enough to fly, it is called a fledgling. Not yet an adult, it stays close to the nest and relies on its parents for food.

All grown up

An adult spotted owlet is small, just 8 inches tall. But it has big, round eyes, which help it see at night.

9

Not just for the birds

Many kinds of animals build nests. Some build them at the tops of trees, some in hollow logs, and others build on or near water. Nests give babies a safe place to live and grow.

Yum!

Paper wasps make nests from plant fiber and wood. They chew up the material, turning it into mush and spitting it out to build the nest. When the babies, called larvae, grow up, they help make the nest bigger.

Walking on water

Jacanas prefer lakes and ponds with lily pads and other plants. Males build nests on the floating plants. They take care of the eggs, then lead their babies (called hatchlings) to find food to eat.

Climb high

People don't build nests, but they like to spend time in trees, too. A tree house is a perfect spot to hang out.

Noisy neighbors

Birds called sociable weavers build huge nests that are like bird apartment houses. Each nest has rooms called cells, and large nests may have up to 100 cells. Other birds take up residence in these nests, too.

Waterfront home

Muskrats build their roomy nests near water, using cattails and other plants. The nest has an underground entrance from a riverbank, like a doorway made from plants that can be removed and replaced when the animals come and go.

Born ready

Go, baby, go! Some babies grow for weeks, months, or years before they can live on their own. Others are ready to walk, swim, or fly right away.

Waddle I do?

These ruddy shelduck ducklings could see, swim, and waddle around right after hatching. They won't be able to fly until they are about two months old.

That's my baby

A black rhino mom has a baby every two to four years. The baby, called a calf, can stand up within ten minutes. It has no horns and stays with mom for protection for about two years.

Flipping out

A mother sea turtle digs a nest and lays about 100 eggs on a sandy beach. When they are born, the babies—called hatchlings—use their little flippers to race to the ocean.

Everyone in the water

Green anacondas can give birth on land or in shallow water. They have 20 to 40 babies at a time. The newborn snakes are about 2 feet long and can swim right away.

Up and at 'em

California quail build nests on the ground. When the chicks hatch, they are ready to move about on their own. These birds roost (sleep) in trees, but prefer walking to flying.

One of a kind

Red panda cubs follow their mothers around, learning to walk along branches and climb trees. This animal has a confusing name—it isn't a panda. It belongs in its own group.

All grown up

Red pandas stretch out on branches to cool off when they're hot. When cold, they wrap their tails around themselves like a blanket.

INFO BITES

Name: Red Panda

Type of animal: Mammal

Home: Found in mountainous regions of Nepal, India, China, Laos, Myanmar, and Bhutan

Baby fact: A red panda mom keeps her babies, called cubs, hidden inside a nest until they're three months old.

SLEEPOVER-WORTHY?

YES   NO

Red pandas like to sleep, spending more than half of each day in slumber. But they sleep high up in slippery trees, and that would be pretty scary!

The **tail** is used for balance and warmth. It will develop rings as the panda cub grows.

Fur is light brown at birth. It gradually darkens as the cub grows up.

Flattened **teeth** are good for chewing bamboo.

Fur on the **soles of the feet** help the panda climb slippery rocks and branches.

A growth from the wrist called a **"panda thumb"** is used to grasp bamboo and other tasty treats.

Mother knows best

Brown bear cubs are born during the winter and spend their first months with mom in her winter den. The furry family emerges when spring comes. The cubs stay with their mother for up to three years, learning everything they need to survive in the wild.

Baby time

How do baby animals survive? Many are taken care of by their parents until they are ready to live on their own.

Taking a bath

This cow is giving her baby its first bath, cleaning the newborn to get it ready for many adventures to come.

Taking turns

Great spotted woodpecker chicks are fed by both of their parents. These youngsters have red feathers on their heads, which are replaced by black feathers when they molt (shed and regrow their feathers).

Got milk?

Just like humans and other mammals, brown bear mothers produce milk for their babies, called cubs. The cubs nurse for a few months, and stay with their mother for two to three years.

Standing up!

Baby giraffes start walking within an hour of birth. When they grow up, they will spend up to 20 hours a day on their feet.

Dog-gone it

A Saint Bernard puppy is born blind. It takes about two weeks for it to open its eyes. At three weeks, it starts to walk. It may start small, but it will grow into a big, lovable adult.

LAP DOG-WORTHY?

☒ YES ☐ NO

This is a loyal and lovable friend. But be prepared to get wet—it drools!

Large **leg muscles** are strong for running and climbing up steep hills or mountains.

INFO BITES

Name: Saint Bernard Dog

Type of animal: Mammal

Home: From Saint Bernard Pass between Italy and Switzerland originally, but now popular as family pets around the world

Baby fact: There are six to eight puppies in a typical Saint Bernard litter. This puppy is tiny at birth, weighing only about 1 pound. It grows quickly—adults weigh up to 200 pounds.

The **coat** can be smooth or rough.

A good **sense of smell** helps sniff out family, friends, and food.

Paws are arched for steady footing.

All grown up

Saint Bernards were once rescue dogs in the snowy Swiss Alps. Now these big dogs make wonderful family pets.

The buddy system

Loving dogs, cats, and even bunnies can be adopted from animal shelters and adoption centers. What kind of pet would you like?

START HERE

◄ Research the type of pet you want.

► Visit an animal shelter or pet adoption center.

▼ Tell the shelter staff what you want.

AT THE SHELTER

A veterinarian (animal doctor) makes sure the animals are healthy and ready to be adopted.

▼ Meet the animals.

Shelters match up people with an animal that is perfect for them.

TAKE YOUR BUDDY HOME!

◄ Once you find the pet for you, your parents need to fill out the adoption papers.

▲ Talk things over as a family.

Handful of cute

At home

Many animals live with people. Some are pets in a classroom or home. Others may live on a family farm. As babies, they are just the right size to cuddle.

Chinchilla

Pig

Tabby cat

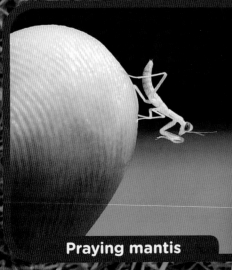
Praying mantis

Sugar glider

Bog turtle

Hamster

Goat

Golden retriever dog

Mountain lion

Rabbit

Squirrel

In the wild

Wild animals know how to live on their own. But some—like an orphaned baby—need human help. Others may be tagged for research so we can learn more about them.

On the spot

Baby spotted eagle rays are called pups. Up to four pups are born in a single litter. When they are born, their fins are rolled up. They unfold and the pup can swim right away.

PLAYFUL PAL?

☐ YES   ☒ NO

Spotted eagle rays are shy, and it's best to leave them alone. You don't want to get close to that dangerous whiplike tail!

Venomous spines on the long **whiplike tail** are used in self-defense.

All grown up
Adults are up to 8 feet long and 10 feet wide. They weigh up to 500 pounds. And they have lots of spots!

Triangular wings called **pectoral fins** help this fish glide through the water.

The **body** is called a disc. The top is covered with spots that may warn others to stay away.

Flat **snout** is used to dig in the sand.

Eyes are positioned on either side of the head to help spot prey and predators.

INFO BITES

Name: Spotted Eagle Ray

Type of animal: Fish

Home: Tropical and coastal waters throughout the world

Baby fact: Pups are born ready to hunt. They look for food under the sand to scoop up in their small mouths.

It's a croc!

"Umph, umph, umph!" When the first crocodile is ready to hatch, it calls out to its siblings. Then each uses its egg tooth—a tough piece of skin on its nose—to break the egg so it can emerge and join the others.

Baby on board

Animal babies know how to travel in style. Some hitch a ride on mom's back, some hold on to the warmth and safety of dad's protective body. All these baby animals stay close to their parents.

Supermom

An orangutan mother and baby have a close bond. They stay together for up to ten years. They often hold hands as they move around.

Hang on!

Three-striped poison frog dads carry their babies (called tadpoles) piggyback style. This way, dad can get around and protect the babies at the same time.

Ride-on gator

An alligator mother nudges her babies into her mouth to carry them to the water. As they get older, they travel on mom's head and snout.

Hairy adventure

As soon as a sloth baby is born, it clings to its mother's hair. It travels that way for at least six months, even after it learns to climb and find food on its own.

Hop on!

Kids hitch rides with their parents, too. A piggyback ride is a fun way to get around.

31

A honey of a bunny

Baby rabbits are called kits or bunnies. Bunnies nurse for eight weeks. The mother's milk is so rich that the bunnies only need to eat once a day.

Strong **back legs** allow the kit to spring forward and land on its **front legs**.

HIGH-MAINTENANCE FRIEND?

[X] YES   [ ] NO

The angora's fur grows quickly and it needs to be brushed often to keep its woolly coat in shape.

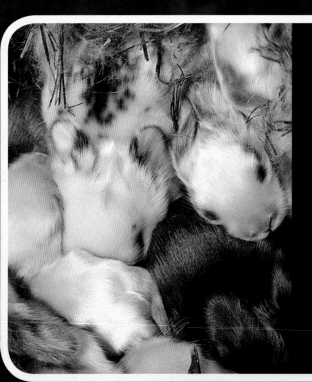

INFO BITES

Name: Angora Rabbit

Type of animal: Mammal

Home: Originally from Angora (now Ankara), Turkey; now found around the world

Baby fact: Angora mothers can give birth to as few as two bunnies to a dozen or more in a litter. The kits stay together for the first few months before they're ready to hop around on their own.

Ears move from side to side, which helps the angora hear noises from any direction.

The **nose** has more than 50 million receptor cells. (Human noses have 6 million.) This bunny can smell a lot!

The soft **coat** is called wool.

All grown up

An adult angora weighs about 5 to 7 pounds. Its ears can be as much as 4 inches high. It can hop and run up to 30 miles an hour.

Dinner's ready

What do baby animals eat? Mammals nurse, which means they start out with milk from their mothers. Eventually, they learn how to find food on their own. Other animals can get their own food from the day they are born.

Bugging out

Tadpoles eat plants in the water. As they grow, they can eat small worms and bugs. As adults, they will catch fast-flying insects with a flick of their long tongues.

Stick with it

A baby giant anteater nurses for about a month. When it gets older, it learns to hunt like its mother. She puts her long, sticky tongue down an ant hole, flicks it around to catch ants, then slurps them up.

Frozen

Baby Weddell seals, called pups, live on the Antarctic ice. A baby nurses for six weeks, then starts hunting with its mother. They eat krill, squid, silverfish, and crabs.

What's mine is yours

Some birds, such as this black-footed albatross, feed their babies by a process called regurgitation. This means the parent partially swallows food, then spits it up for the chick to eat.

Peek-a-boo

Marsupials are animals that raise their young in pouches. A marsupial baby is not fully developed when it is born. It crawls to its mother's pouch after birth. There, it nurses and grows until it's ready for life on the outside.

POUCH LIVING

There are two kinds of pouches. Some animals, such as kangaroos, have front-facing pouches. This means the pouches open at the top. Animals that dig burrows have rear-facing pouches. These pouches open on the bottom, which protects the babies from flying dirt.

Virginia opossum

Mom gives birth to six or more bee-sized babies. They make the great climb to her front-facing pouch. After three months, they are ready to come out.

Sugar glider

A sugar glider gives birth to one or two joeys. They live inside her front-facing pouch for about two months. When they leave the pouch, they share a family nest with other babies for a few months.

Common wombat

This joey stays in the pouch for nine months. Mom's pouch is rear-facing, so her joey won't get dirt in its eyes when she digs. It can peek out while she's digging.

Kangaroo

A grey kangaroo baby (called a joey) spends nine months in mom's pouch. After it comes out, it returns to nurse for a few months, even if there's another baby inside. To keep things tidy, mom sticks her snout into the pouch and cleans it with her tongue.

Love shows the way

Animal families show their love, just as human families do. Sharing food, helping each other, and playing are all things animal families do together.

Practice sessions

Red foxes learn to stalk and pounce to get food. They also help care for their younger brothers and sisters. They bring them food—or even a fun toy to play with.

Lifesaver

Some animals care for their families by protecting them. Male African bullfrogs stand over their tadpoles while they are in the water, chasing away any animal that comes too close.

Cooperation

Common vampire bat females form close bonds. Small groups roost (sleep) together, and help care for and groom each other's pups (baby bats).

Getting ready for baby

Few animal parents prepare for their young like clownfish do. Dad cleans the eggs before they hatch. Both parents use their fins to fan the orange-colored eggs to provide oxygen-rich water. This helps give the little ones a better chance to survive.

BFFs

Brothers and sisters are great teachers. They can help you learn new things.

Bedazzle this!

A baby planthopper is called a nymph. This tiny 1/8-inch long insect hatches from an egg. It is born without wings. Its legs have toothless gears that help it hop from place to place. As it grows up, it loses these gears and grows wings for flight.

Sparkly, colorful **tail-like growths** fan out to distract predators.

HOPSCOTCH-WORTHY?

☒ ☐
YES NO

Planthopper nymphs can jump far for an animal the size of a pencil eraser. They can hop a distance of about 3 feet.

Mouth parts suck sap and juices from plants and fruits.

INFO BITES

Name: Planthopper

Type of animal: Insect

Home: Worldwide

Baby fact: A flatid planthopper starts out as an egg. When it emerges, it is white and fuzzy.

Hind legs have toothlike gears for jumping.

Tymbals on the belly vibrate, making sounds to communicate with others.

All grown up

Adult planthoppers don't look like the nymphs. They lose their shiny tails and grow wings for flight.

Going my way?

Snails are some of the slowest animals on Earth. With only one foot, they travel less than a mile in an hour. They produce a slimy goo that helps them slide along any surface. Young snails may hitch a ride to get around.

Making changes

Some animal babies don't look the same as they will when they are adults. Different animals change in different ways.

Fuzzy wuzzy

Black swan babies, called cygnets, are born with soft, pale down. By the time they are five or six months old, their black feathers grow in and they can fly. Just like their parents, their wing feathers will be white.

I can't seal you

Harp seals are born to blend in to their icy home. When they are about three weeks old, they begin to shed their white fur. Their new coat is gray with spots—just like their parents'!

Awesome Aussies

Emu chicks have brown and white stripes that help them blend into their Australian surroundings. The stripes fade after a few months. At a year old, they are full grown.

Growing pains

A young tarantula hatches from an egg. It doesn't have a skeleton inside its body; it has a hard outer shell called an exoskeleton. It sheds its exoskeleton to grow.

L'il blue eyes

Bobcat kittens have bright blue eyes that become green or golden brown by the time the kittens are adults. They will grow a ruff of long fur around their necks, too.

Carrot top

Spectacled leaf monkey babies have bright orange or yellow fur at first. This may help the mothers keep an eye on them in the dark, leafy trees where they live.

Scent-sational!

Baby skunks, called kits, weigh only 7 ounces at birth. That's about what a softball weighs. They are blind and hairless. At eight days old, kits can produce an odor called musk. At about three weeks, they can open their eyes. Stand back—at this age, they can also release a full stinky spray.

The **tail** is raised to expose scent glands when spraying.

INFO BITES

Name: Striped Skunk

Type of animal: Mammal

Home: Southern Canada, United States, and northern Mexico

Baby fact: When a mother skunk is getting ready to have her babies, she looks for a safe place. She may choose another animal's unused den, or a hollowed-out tree or log.

GOOD PICNIC PAL?

☒ YES ☒ NO

Skunks are omnivores, which means they'll eat almost anything. But eww, that smell!

Black-and-white **striped fur** warns predators to avoid this stinker.

A good **sense of smell** helps with nighttime hunting.

Powerful **front feet** and long **claws** are used for digging.

All grown up

Striped skunks can grow to 1 1/2 feet long and weigh up to 10 pounds, about the size of a housecat.

47

Egg-cellent

Birds

Baby birds use an egg tooth, a bump on the beak, to break out of the eggshell. Some are fuzzy or feathered, while others are born naked.

Steppe eagle

Eurasian coot

Buff Orpington chicken

Flamboyant cuttlefish

Brown trout

Five-lined skink

American robin

Mallard duck

Peacock

Green sea turtle

Common frog tadpole

Shield bug

Other hatchlings

Sea turtles begin as eggs buried in the sand. Fish emerge from eggs underwater. Others—such as insects, spiders, and reptiles—hatch from eggs, too.

The stackup

TALENT: TAKING ITS TIME

This amphibian has large babies that grow slowly. After quickly hatching from its egg, a tadpole can take up to three years to become an adult frog.

american bullfrog

At hatching: Up to 6 inches long

TALENT: SHOWING OFF

Peachicks (baby peacocks) can walk, eat, and drink on their own. And at six months, male peachicks get more colorful feathers. They won't have a full rainbow-hued tail until they are three years old.

peacock

At hatching: About 4 inches tall

hippopotamus

At birth: About 4 feet long and up to 100 pounds

TALENT: WATER HOPPING

A baby hippo is born underwater. Its mother pushes it to the surface for its first breath. Hippos can't swim. These mammals move through the water by hopping along the bottom.

orca

At birth: About 8 1/2 feet long and up to 350 pounds

TALENT: GETTING BIG

Orca calves nurse dozens of times a day, for a few seconds up to a minute at a time. In their first year, they grow about 2 feet and gain 800 pounds.

TALENT: CUDDLING

Polar bear cubs are born in a snow den. They grow quickly. When they leave the den three months later, they weigh about 30 pounds.

polar bear

At birth: About 12 inches long and up to 1 ½ pounds

TALENT: STANDING TALL

Giraffe mothers give birth standing up. The baby, called a calf, falls about six feet to the ground. The impact helps it start breathing. Its mother cleans it off, and within minutes the calf is up and walking.

giraffe

At birth: About 6 feet tall and 150 pounds

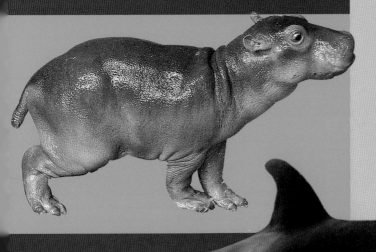

The sister and brother act

Just like human brothers and sisters, these animal siblings like to hang out together. They sometimes argue and fight, too. But mostly they play, hunt, and explore.

Wrestlemania

Brown bear cubs climb, wrestle, and play fight. They have staring contests and roll around in the dirt. When they stand on their back legs and box, they are learning to show their power.

Taking care of business

Naked mole rat families live in groups called colonies. At the head of each colony is a queen. She has up to 50 babies a year. These animals have sharp front teeth. They use them to dig tunnels underground.

Sweet sis

All the worker bees in a honey bee hive are sisters. When they are young, they take care of the hive and keep it clean. The older ones collect pollen from flowers and bring it to the hive.

Knock a croc

Head butting, biting, sneak attacks, and tail whipping? That's how crocodile brothers and sisters practice their survival skills. Sometimes they end up in a sibling pile-up.

Playtime!

Sisters and brothers are built-in playmates. You can hang out together, play, and learn from one another, too.

Claw-some cutie

Maine coon babies are called kittens. At three weeks, they begin to explore. If they wander too far, mom lets them know. She has a special call they recognize. These playful cats act like kittens even when they grow up.

INFO BITES

Name: Maine Coon Cat

Type of animal: Mammal

Home: Originally from Maine; now a popular family pet found around the world

Baby fact: These kittens are super fluffy. They don't have an outer coat (called guard hairs) yet.

All grown up
Adults grow to more than 3 feet long and weigh up to about 18 pounds. The lionlike mane around the neck grows very long and fluffy.

PURR-FECT PAL?

☒ YES ☐ NO

These cats are sometimes shy around strangers, but they are friendly, smart, and loyal.

Ears are large, wide at the bottom, and have tufts of fur.

A long, bushy **tail** helps with balance and wraps around the cat's body for warmth.

Fur coat is water resistant, useful for staying dry and warm.

Oversized **paws** act like snowshoes.

Solos and siblings

Singletons

Some animals, including many mammals, have one baby at a time. They need months or even years to learn all they need to know to live on their own.

African elephant

Emperor penguin

Humpback whale

Meerkat

Dwarf Hotot rabbit

Ostrich

Mountain gorilla

Jersey cow

Hippopotamus

Red fox

Spider wasp

Pig

Multiples

Many animals have more than one baby at a time. Cats, dogs, bunnies, and pigs have litters. Birds, amphibians, and reptiles lay clutches of eggs.

Mini me

Some baby animals look like small versions of their parents.

A capybara baby, called a pup, looks like its parents when it is born, and it can move like them, too.

Great horned owl babies, called owlets, look so much like mom that they can hide in plain sight.

Golden lion tamarin babies ride on dad's back between feedings.

A baby burro, called a foal, can stand and nurse within 30 minutes.

It looks like mini-mom, but this baby camel, called a calf, won't be an adult until it is five years old.

Ornate ghost pipefish are born able to swim freely and feed themselves.

A baby porcupine is called a porcupette. Its quills are soft when it is born.

Baby Texas horned lizards have spines on their heads. More spines grow along their bodies over time.

Warthog piglets are born in a burrow. They start exploring at about two weeks, but stay close to their mother.

When the southern river terrapin hatches from its egg, it moves straight to the water.

Mountain goat babies, called kids, are born in rocky areas, and can stand up right away.

A newborn saiga antelope calf migrates (travels) with its mother and herd to a summer feeding area.

Prairie dogs live in family groups, which means babies, called pups, have plenty of playmates.

Coastal brown bear cubs like to explore. When it is naptime, their mother stays nearby.

It takes about three months for a Galápagos marine iguana to hatch from its egg.

Hiding out

Animals need a safe place to have their babies. Some build permanent homes. Others find temporary shelter in hollow logs or snowy dens.

Prairie dog

Prairie dogs live in large underground colonies called towns, made up of lots of smaller burrows. There are rooms used for storing food and standing guard. Females give birth to litters of one to eight pups in nesting rooms.

Hare today, gone tomorrow

A female cottontail rabbit, called a doe, builds a shallow nest for her babies. She lines it with grass, leaves, and fur. Baby cottontails stay in the nest for about two weeks, then they are able to move about on their own.

Always moving

Bobcats move around a lot and have several homes. A hollow log or tree can become a birth den for a mother and her babies. Tree stumps, brush, or rock piles can be used as a shelter.

Cozy warm

When a female polar bear is pregnant, she digs out a snow den. She will give birth there. She keeps her cubs in the snow den until they are old enough to walk across the ice to fish.

Hideaway

All you need is a tent, a book, and a reading light. You can hide out, too!

A masked bandit

A baby northern raccoon is called a kit. It has a distinctive black mask and faint tail-ring markings. These become more pronounced as the kit grows older. When it is three months old, it begins to explore beyond the den.

GOOD STUDY BUDDY?

☐ YES ☒ NO

Raccoons are smart, but they're noisy. They hiss, growl, and scream.

Bushy **tail** is up to half the raccoon's length and has 5 to 8 light-colored rings.

All grown up

Raccoons will climb almost anyplace to get food. They most often climb trees—to sleep, to have babies, and to avoid danger.

Black mask around **eyes** may help deflect light.

Front paws and **claws** are used to grasp food, catch fish, and even open doors.

INFo BITES

Name: Northern Raccoon

Type of animal: Mammal

Home: Native to North America, Central America, now found in some parts of Europe and Japan

Baby fact: Kits need to develop good skills for tree climbing. Oops! This one needs a little practice.

Turning things around

Conservation means preserving, protecting, or restoring a natural place, thing, or animal. About 30 years ago, there were fewer than three dozen black-footed ferrets alive in the wild. Today, 150 to 200 are released into the wild each year. How did this change happen? Scientists, government agencies, and ordinary citizens teamed up to save the species.

► Doctors and staff look after the kits and make sure they are healthy.

▲ Baby ferrets, called kits, are bred and raised in the center.

▼ Kits learn how to pop up through holes. They will spend 90% of their adult lives underground.

START HERE
Black-footed ferret conservation center

◄ Conservation center staff and residents work together to release the ferrets into the wild.

HOME!

High mountain prairie
Historical range
Reintroduction sites

▲ Their native habitat is the North American prairie, where winters can be cold.

Black-footed ferrets are the only ferret species native to North America. To learn more, visit blackfootedferret.org

► They spend a month in a preconditioning pen, where they get used to living outdoors.

▲ They move to a pen that is like a small prairie-dog town. In the wild, they hunt prairie dogs for food.

Special tail-ent

Virginia opossums have prehensile tails—tails they can use to grip branches for balance or to carry leaves. But only baby opossums hang from their tails. The adults are too heavy for their tails to support them.

Family ties

Like human parents, many animals teach their babies how to find food and shelter, and protect themselves.

Full of pride

Lions live in large family groups called prides. The females, called lionesses, hunt and raise their babies, called cubs, together. Males guard the territory.

Nest mates

Bald eagle parents build a nest together. They take turns caring for their baby eaglets. The parents stay together for life. Their offspring (children) return to nest in the same area.

Moms rule

An African elephant family is made up of closely related females and their babies, called calves. It is led by an older female called the matriarch (head of the family). They form lifelong friendships and show affection.

Forever family

Orcas live in groups called pods. These groups can range from a few to as many as 100 orcas. When a calf (baby orca) is born, the aunts and sisters help push it to the surface to breathe.

Dad's in charge

Grauer's gorilla families are called troops. Members of the troop take turns caring for the babies, which are called infants. Starting at about seven years old, the young gorillas move on to start their own families.

Love for life

It is rare to see a French angelfish alone. When these fish pair up, it's for life. They travel and hunt together. They protect each other and their young.

Loyally yours

Gray wolves, also called timber wolves, make lifetime bonds. They stick together—a wolf pack consists of a male, a female, and their young. If there is enough food in the area, a lone wolf may be allowed to join the pack.

Otter-ly adorable

A mother sea otter fluffs up her baby's fur with her tongue. This keeps the baby, called a pup, warm and dry. It also makes it buoyant, which means it can float. At four weeks old, the pup learns to swim. It also starts to eat food, like clams and crabs, that its mother finds for it.

INFO BITES

Name: Sea Otter

Type of animal: Mammal

Home: Most live in Alaskan waters. They are also found in the coastal waters of the Pacific Ocean in North America and Asia.

Baby fact: When she hunts for food, a mother wraps her pup in kelp (thick seaweed) so it doesn't drift out to sea.

Back feet are used like flippers for swimming.

SWIM BUDDY-WORTHY?

YES   NO

Sea otters spend most of their time in the water. Their fur keeps them warm, and they are excellent divers.

Long whiskers help locate food.

Two layers of **fur** trap air to keep skin dry.

All grown up
Sea otters float on their backs when sleeping. They sleep in a group and often hold paws so they don't drift apart.

Habitat habits

A habitat is a place where an animal or plant lives. There are different habitats around the world, and different ways baby animals live in them.

PUFFIN STUFF

The Atlantic puffin spends most of its time at sea. Its waterproof feathers keep it warm in its tundra home. At nesting time, when it may be spotted further south, it digs a long, narrow burrow in a rocky cliff. A baby puffin, called a puffling, uses one area of the burrow as its bathroom. This helps it keep its feathers clean.

BABY BELUGA

The Arctic Ocean is home for beluga whales. They swim in groups called pods. Babies, called calves, are born in the late spring or summer. They

BREAKING OUT

Desert tortoises live in the dry, hot desert. When a hatchling breaks out of its egg, it is about 2 inches long. How quickly it grows depends on how much water and food are available.

MOM AND ME

Zebras live in big herds on the grasslands. But a mother keeps her newborn foal away from the group at first. She makes sure her baby recognizes her sound, look, and smell before letting other zebras near.

BIG EATER

Tiger salamander babies (called larvae) are born underwater in a wetland habitat. They eat insects, worms, and frogs, and grow up to 5 inches long.

YOU CAN, TOUCAN

Toucans use their large beaks to pluck fruit from branches in their rain forest habitat. But baby toucans have small beaks, so their parents feed them for the first few months.

learn what they need to know to survive by watching and copying members of the pod.

Baby animal activities

WHAT'S MY NAME?

A baby horse is called a foal and a baby cow is called a calf. Can you match these animals with their correct baby names?

BABY NAMES

PEACHICK
KIT
PIGLET
PORCUPETTE
PINKIE

ANSWERS: 1. A baby mouse is called a pinkie. 2. A baby porcupine is called a porcupette. 3. A baby skunk is called a kit. 4. A baby peacock is called a peachick. 5. A baby hedgehog is called a piglet.

DRESS YOUR NEST

Some baby animals start their lives in a nest lined with soft materials such as grasses or fur. Make a nest for one of your toys with crafting and household items.

What you'll need:
- 1 paper bowl
- 1 sheet brown tissue paper
- Kids' school glue
- Cotton balls, yarn, and other soft items

1. Crinkle the tissue paper into a ball, then flatten it out. Wrap it around the bowl to form a nest.

2. Put dots of glue on the tissue paper lining the bowl.

3. Attach cotton balls, pom poms, and yarn to the glue to make a soft lining.

BABY STEPS

Baby animals need time to grow into their amazing abilities. See how different baby animals move around in this fun game.

What you'll need:
- 2 pieces of string, each about 6 feet long
- At least 2 players
- 1 person to be the timer

1. Stretch out a piece of string on the floor to be your starting point.

2. Take 10 steps forward and stretch out the second piece of string. This will be the finish line.

3. Choose an animal shown here.

4. Line up together.

5. When the timer calls "Go," move the way your baby animal does. The first baby animal to the finish line wins!

Try being a different animal next time and see which baby animals move fastest.

Hop!

Bunnies take quick, short hops before they can run.

Flap!

Tern chicks flap their wings and walk before they can fly.

Waddle!

Penguin chicks waddle, which means they rock side to side while walking. They take small steps with their short legs.

Crawl!

Sea turtles use their flippers to crawl along the sand to the ocean.

74

Resources

FIND OUT MORE

Learn more about baby animals by reading books, checking out interesting websites, and visiting zoos and museums.

PLACES TO VISIT

UNITED STATES

Aquarium of the Pacific
Long Beach, CA
aquariumofpacific.org
The Aquarium of the Pacific features 19 major habitats and is home to more than 11,000 ocean animals. Check out the shark lagoons and stingray pools, or take a whale watching cruise. Baby animals born at the zoo include harbor seal pups, otter pups, and penguin chicks.

Sacramento Zoo
Sacramento, CA
saczoo.org
There are more than 500 animals to see and learn about at the Sacramento Zoo. Exotic baby and adult animals include red river hoglets and Masai giraffes. Nighttime starlight and family overnight Safaris feature nocturnal animals in action.

San Diego Zoo
San Diego, CA
zoo.sandiegozoo.org
Walk the Monkey, Hippo, and Tiger Trails to see these amazing animals at the San Diego Zoo. And check out the Animal Care center at the Nairobi Village exhibit, where orphaned or injured baby animals like impalas and markhor goats are taken care of by zookeepers and other animals that take care of orphaned babies.

Smithsonian's National Zoo
Washington, DC
nationalzoo.si.edu
See more than 1,500 animals from 300 different species at the National Zoo. Visitors can see an elusive sand cat in the Small Mammals House and giant pandas on the Asia Trail. Walk the Cheetah Conservation Trail and visit the Kid's Farm.

Lion Country Safari
Loxahatchee, FL
lioncountrysafari.com
Take a drive through Lion Country Safari to watch wild animals on the move, including African lions, wildebeests, impalas, and ostriches. Baby animals born here include giraffe and antelope calves.

Indianapolis Zoo
Indianapolis, IN
indianapoliszoo.com
The Indianapolis Zoo is a zoo, an aquarium, and a botanical garden, which means you can see all kinds of animals and plants in different exhibits. Babies born at the zoo include lion cubs, giraffe calves, and meerkat pups.

Bronx Zoo
Bronx, NY
bronxzoo.com
The Bronx Zoo offers opportunities to get up close and personal with some of the animals. You can feed goats in the farmyard area, or even ride a camel! Baby animals born at the zoo include markhor goat kids, penguin chicks, and Malayan tiger cubs.

Columbus Zoo and Aquarium
Powell, OH
columbuszoo.org
The Animal Encounters Village at the Columbus Zoo lets you get up close with some of its 7,000 animals. In 2016, the zoo welcomed Nora—the first polar bear born and raised at the Columbus Zoo since the opening of the Polar Frontier exhibit.

Philadelphia Zoo
Philadelphia, PA
philadelphiazoo.org
The Philadelphia Zoo features The KidZooU, a children's zoo and wildlife academy. The children's zoo offers opportunities to see animals up close, groom them, and learn about conservation. Baby animals born at the zoo include gorillas and lemurs.

Houston Zoo
Houston, TX
houstonzoo.org
The Houston Zoo offers private tours during which visitors go behind the scenes to see animal feedings and visit the zoo's animal hospital, where zoo babies and injured animals are cared for. Baby animals born at the zoo include copperhead snakes, bush vipers, a Victoria crowned pigeon chick, and a Gerenuk gazelle calf.

San Antonio Zoo
San Antonio, TX
sazoo-aq.org
This zoo is home to a wide variety of animals representing 750 species. There are specialized education adventures and opportunities to see the newest baby animals. Babies born at the zoo include a tree kangaroo joey, a litter of lion cubs, and flamingo chicks.

CANADA

Calgary Zoo
Calgary, AB
calgaryzoo.com
There are daily special events at the Calgary Zoo, where you can check out the otters, tigers, and snow leopards during feeding times and see how the keepers care for porcupines, giraffes, and camels. Baby animals born at the zoo include a gorilla infant, an elephant calf, and a baby giraffe.

Toronto Zoo
Toronto, ON
torontozoo.com
Toronto Zoo exhibits include the African Savanna and Tundra Trek. Baby animals born at the zoo include a rhino calf, polar bear cub, gorilla, and giant panda cub. The Discovery Zone features a Kids' Zoo, and you can learn about endangered species when you ride the Conservation Carousel.

WEBSITES

You can visit all of the zoos and animal centers online to learn more. Here are some additional websites to check out.

discoverykids.com
Check out baby rattlesnakes and other animals in the wild. Round up all the baby meerkats when you play Catch the Pups. Fun activities and videos introduce kids to all kinds of animals at this entertainment site.

National Park Service
nps.gov
You can see all kinds of wildlife, from wolves in Yellowstone (Wyoming) and manatees in the Everglades (Florida) to spotted owls in Yosemite (California) and beavers in Acadia (Maine) in our National Parks. Visit the website to learn about the different parks and animals that live there, and find cool photos and activities. You can even become a Junior Ranger and learn to explore and protect our natural world.

BOOKS

ANIMAL BITES
Meet amazing animals from around the world in these *Animal Bites* books:

Animals On The Move
Explore different ways animals move, from running and flying to hopping, swimming, and slithering. Learn why animals move the way they do, and the many special abilities they have to get around.

Farm Animals
Take a trip to the farm. Learn about farm life, and see how and where farm animals live.

Ocean Animals
Journey through the oceans. Learn about marine animals from around the world, and see how and where they live.

Polar Animals
Travel from the tippy-top of the planet to the very bottom. Learn about the animals that call the North and South Poles home, and see how and where they live.

Wild Animals
Explore the habitats of wild animals around the world. Learn about animals that survive and thrive in the wild, and see how and where they live.

ANIMAL PLANET
ANIMAL ATLAS
What is a habitat? What is a food web? Answers to these and hundreds of other questions are answered in a kid-friendly way.

ANIMALS: A VISUAL
ENCYCLOPEDIA
Meet more than 2,500 amazing animals in this comprehensive family reference book. It includes more than 1,000 stunning photos!

Glossary

amphibian A cold-blooded animal that starts its life in the water but lives most of its adult life on land.

Antarctic Relating to the South Pole.

Arctic Relating to the North Pole.

breeding The process of mating and producing babies.

burrow A home animals make by tunneling into the ground.

▼ **buoyant** Able to float.

*A sea otter pup's thick coat helps make it **buoyant.***

calf The young of some animals. Baby cows, elephants, and whales are called calves.

captive An animal that lives in an enclosed, protected place rather than in the wild.

chrysalis A hard, protective case that covers the pupa of a butterfly during metamorphosis.

▼ **clutch** A group of eggs laid by a bird, amphibian, or reptile.

*When a **clutch** of Nile crocodiles is ready to hatch, the hatchlings call to one another and their mother from inside their eggs.*

coat The hair or fur that covers an animal.

cocoon The silky covering a moth larva spins around itself during metamorphosis.

colony A group of animals living in one place. Naked mole rats live in colonies.

conservation The protection of animals, plants, and natural resources.

cub A baby tiger, bear, or one of several other types of animals.

den A small, hollowed area where an animal lives. Bears live in dens.

desert Dry land that receives very little rainfall.

down Soft, fluffy feathers that cover some baby birds.

▼ **egg case** A soft pouch that protects the eggs of some animals.

*Most catsharks lay **egg cases.***

foal A baby horse or zebra.

grassland A field that is mostly covered with grass, often used as a pasture for animals.

habitat The place where an animal usually lives, or an area where different animals live together.

hatch To break out of an egg, chrysalis, or pupa. Birds, insects, and some reptiles hatch.

hatchlings Baby animals that have hatched from eggs.

herd A group of animals that live or are kept together. Antelope live in herds.

joey A baby marsupial, such as a sugar glider, or wombat.

krill A type of zooplankton. Krill are like tiny shrimp.

kit A name for certain baby animals. Baby raccoons and rabbits are called kits.

larva The baby, wormlike form of animals that go through complete metamorphosis. A caterpillar is the larva of a butterfly.

*Pigs have about 10 piglets in a **litter**.*

▲ **litter** A group of baby animals born at the same time to the same mother.

mammal An animal that produces milk to feed its young, has hair on its body, and has a backbone. Humans, cows, and horses are mammals.

marsupial An animal that raises its young in a pouch on the mother's belly. Kangaroos, opossums, and wombats are marsupials.

metamorphosis The three- or four-stage process of changing from an egg to an adult. Insects and most amphibians go through metamorphosis.

musk A strong-smelling substance produced by some animals. Skunks spray musk.

nurse To drink milk from the mother. Baby mammals nurse.

nymph The young form of an insect that goes through simple metamorphosis. A baby praying mantis is a nymph.

pectoral fin The front fin of fish and other marine animals.

pollen A yellow, powdery substance in flowers that helps them reproduce. Bees collect pollen to make honey.

pouch A pocket of skin on the belly of female marsupials. The babies live in the mother's pouch after they are born.

prairie A large, flat area of land with few or no trees that is mostly covered with tall grasses.

predator An animal that hunts and eats other animals.

prey An animal that is eaten by other animals.

pup A baby wolf, hamster, spotted eagle ray, or one of several other types of baby animals.

pupa The form a baby insect takes in the third stage of complete metamorphosis.

queen The most important female in some groups of animals. Bees have a queen.

rain forest A forest, typically found in tropical areas, that gets heavy rainfall.

receptor cells Tissue in the body that can sense changes around it, such as scent or light. Noses and eyes have receptor cells.

reptile A cold-blooded animal that often has scales. Snakes and alligators are reptiles.

spawn The eggs of some animals that live in the water. Fish produce spawn.

*Reindeer, also called caribou, live in the Arctic **tundra**.*

▲ **tundra** Flat land in the Arctic region. No trees can grow there, and the ground is always frozen.

tymbal Vibrating tissue on the belly of certain insects that helps them make sounds. Planthoppers communicate with their tymbals.

venomous Producing venom as protection from predators or kill prey.

wetland Land that is mostly covered with shallow water.

Index

Illustrations are indicated by **boldface.** When illustrations fall within a page span, the entire span of pages is **boldface.**

A

Adoption 22–23
African bullfrogs 38, **38**
African elephants **56,** 68, **68**
Alligators 31, **31**
American bullfrogs 50, **50**
American robins **49**
Amphibians 30, **30,** 34, **34,** 38, **38, 49–50,** 50, 57, 73, **73**
Angora rabbits 32–33, **32–33**
Animal conservation centers 64–65, **64–65**
Animal groupings 52, 60, 68–69. *See also* Families
Animal research 25
Animal shelters and pet adoption centers 22–23, **22–23**
Ants 34

B

Bald eagles 68, **68**
Bathing 18–19
Bears 16, **16–17,** 19, **19,** 51–52, **51–52,** 59, **59,** 61, **61**
Beluga whales 72–73, **72–73**
Birds
    beaks 8–9, 48, 73
    care by parents 10, 18, 68, **68**
    color and appearance 18, 44–45, **44–45,** 48–50, **48–50,** 58, 73
    development of chicks 8–9, **8–9,** 12–13, 49–50, **50,** 56–57, 72–73
    feathers 8, 18, 44–45, 48, 72
    food and feeding habits 10, 18, **18,** 35, **35,** 73
    nesting 8, 10–11, **11,** 13, 68, 72
Birth
    from eggs 6–7, 29, 40, 48–50
    litter size 20, 26, 32, 57, 60
    live 13, 36–37, 46, 51, 56–57
    shelters for 60–61
Black
footed albatross 35, **35**
Black-footed ferrets 64–65, **64–65**
Black rhinoceros 12, **12**
Black swans 44, **44**
Bobcats 45, **45,** 61, **61**
Bog turtles **24**
Brown bears 16, **16–17,** 19, **19,** 52, **52,** 59, **59**
Brown trout 48
Buff Orpington chickens 48

Burros 58, **58**
Burrows 36, 59–60, 72. *See also* Homes
Butterflies 7, **7**

C

California quail 13, **13**
Calves 12, 58, 72
Camel 58, **58**
Capybaras 58, **58**
Caterpillar 7, **7**
Cats 22–23, **22–24,** 54–55, **54–55,** 57, 61
Chinchillas **24**
Chrysalis 7, **7**
Clownfish 39, **39**
Cocoons 6–7
Color
    and growth 15, 18, 44–45, 50, 62–63
    as protection 26–27, 41, 45, 47, 58
Common frogs **49**
Common vampire bats 38, **38**
Common wombats 36, **36**
Conservation 64–65
Cooperation in groups 38, 52, 60, 68–69. *See also* Families
Coral reefs 6, **6–7**
Cottontail rabbits 60, **60**
Cows 18, **18,** 57
Crocodiles 28–29, **28–29,** 53, **53**
Cubs 14–16, 19, 51–52, 59, 61, 68
Cygnets 44, **44**

D

Dens 16, 60. *See also* Homes
Desert tortoises 72, **72**
Dogs 20–23, **20–23, 25,** 57
Duck-billed platypus 6, **6**
Ducks 12, **12,** 49
Dwarf Hotot rabbits 56

E

Ears and hearing 33, 55
Eggs 6–7, 29, 40, **48–49,** 48–50, 57
Egg tooth 8, 29, 48
Emperor penguins 56
Emus 45, **45**
Eurasian coots 48
Exoskeletons 45
Eyes and vision 8–9, 20, 27, 45–46, 63

F

Families
    care and protection by 9, 12–14, 16, 18–19, 30–31, 38–39, 54, 56–57, 68–69
    learning and sharing in 38–39, 52–53, 68–69
Feathers 8, 18, 44–45, 48, 72
Feet, paws, and claws 15, **15,** 21, **21,** 47, **47,** 55, **55,** 63, **63,** 70–71, **70–71**

Fins and flippers 13, 26–27
Fish 26–27, 39, **39, 48,** 58, **58,** 63, 69, **69**
Five-lined skink **48**
Flamboyant cuttlefish **48**
Fledglings 9
Flying 8–9, 12–13, 40–41, 44
Foals 58
Food and feeding habits
    hunting 27, 34–35, 47, 65, 68–70
    nursing 19, 32, 34–37, 50, 58
    plants as 10, 15, 41, 53, 73
French angelfish 69, **69**
Frogs 30, **30,** 38, **38, 49–50,** 50, 73
Fur and hair 15–16, 21, 31, 33, 45, 47, 54–55, 70–71

G

Galápagos marine iguanas 59, **59**
Ghost pipefish 58, **58**
Giant anteaters 34, **34**
Giraffes 19, **19,** 51, **51**
Goats 25
Golden lion tamarins 58, **58**
Golden retrievers **25**
Government conservation 64–65
Grauer's gorillas 69, **69**
Gray wolves 69, **69**
Great horned owls 58, **58**
Great spotted woodpeckers 18, **18**
Green anacondas 13, **13**
Green sea turtles **49**
Grey kangaroos 37, **37**
Grooming 38
Growth rates 6–7, 10–13, 18–20, 32, 36–37, 50–51, 54, 56, 72

H

Habitats
    beaches and oceans 13, 50, 70, 72
    definition 72
    desert and tundra 72
    forest, prairie, and grasslands 60–61, 65, 73
    lakes and rivers 10–11, 59
    mountains 21, 59
    polar snow den 51, 61
    and temperature 14, 55, 72
    tropics and rain forests 27, 73
    underground 60, 64–65
Hamsters **25**
Harp seals 45, **45**
Herds 73
Hibernation 16
Hippopotamus 50, **51, 57**
Hives 53
Homes
    birthing shelters 60–61
    burrows 36, 52, 59–60, 72
    dens and hives 16, 53, 60
    nests 9–11, **10–11,** 13–14, 60, 68, 72, 74

Honey bees 53, **53**
Horns 12
Humpback whales **56**
Hunting 47, 65, 68-69

I

Insects 7, **7**, 10, **10**, 34, 40-41, **40-41**, 45, **45**, 49, **49**, 53, **53, 57**

J

Jacanas 10, **10**
Jersey cows **57**
Joeys 36-37

K

Kangaroos 37, **37**
Kits 32-33, 46, 62-64

L

Larvae 7, **7**, 10
Legs 32, 40-41
Lions 68, **68**
Love 38-39

M

Maine Coon cats 54-55, **54-55**
Mallard ducks 49
Mammals 6, 11-12, 14-15, 18-20, 32-35, 46, 54, 56-57, 63, 70
Marsupials 36-37, **36-37**
Mating 68-69
Matriarch 68
Meerkats **56**
Metamorphosis 7
Migration 59
Molting 18
Monarch butterflies 7, **7**
Mountain goats 59, **59**
Mountain gorillas **57**
Mountain lions **25**
Musk 46
Muskrats 11, **11**

N

Naked mole rats 52, **52**
Native species 65
Nests 9-11, **10-11**, 13-14, 60, 68, 72, 74. *See also* Homes
Northern raccoons 62-63, **62-63**
Nursing 19, 32, 34-37, 50, 58
Nymphs 7, 40

O

Oceans 6, 13
Omnivores 47
Orangutans 30, **30**
Orcas 50, **51**, 68-69, **68-69**
Orphaned animals 25
Ostriches **56**
Owls 8-9, **8-9**, 58, **58**

P

Paper wasps 10, **10**
Parents
    and appearance of babies 44-45, 58-59
    care and protection by 9, 12-14, 16, 18-19, 30-31, 38-39, 54, 56-57, 68-69
Peacocks **49**, 50, **50**
Pet adoption and animal shelters 22-23, **22-23**
Pets 20-25, **22-23**, 32, 54
Pigs **24**, 57, **57**
Planthoppers 40-41, **40-41**
Plants 10-11, 15, 53, 73
Playing 38, 52-53, 59
Pods 69, 72
Polar bears 51, **51**, 61, **61**
Porcupines 59, **59**
Prairie dogs 59-60, **59-60**, 65
Praying mantises 7, **7**, 24
Protection 9, 12-14, 16, 18-19, 30-31, 38-39, 54, 68-69
Puffins 72, **72**
Puffling 72
Pups 26-27, 38, 58

Q

Queens 52

R

Rabbits 22-23, **22-23, 25**, 32-33, **32-33**, 56, 57
Raccoons 62-63, **62-63**
Red foxes 38, **39, 57**
Red pandas 14-15, **14-15**
Reptiles 13, **13, 24**, 28-29, **28-29**, 31, **31**, 49, **49**, 53, **53**, 59, **59**, 72, **72**
Rescue dogs 21
Roosting 13, 38
Ruddy shelducks 12, **12**

S

Saiga antelopes 59, **59**
Saint Bernard dogs 20-21, **20-21**
School and classroom pets 24-25
Scientific research 64-65
Sea otters 70-71, **70-71**
Seasonal behavior 16
Sea turtles 13, **13,** 49
Shelter. *See* homes
Shield bugs **49**
Siblings 39, **39**, 52-53. *See also* Families
Size and weight
    adult 20, 26, 33, 47
    babies 24, 50-51
    growth rates 6-7, 10-13, 18-20, 32, 36-37, 54, 56, 72
Skunks 46-47, **46-47**
Sleeping 12-15, 38

Sloths 31, **31**
Smell and scent 21, 33, 46-47, 73
Snails 42-43, **42-43**
Snakes 13, **13**
Snouts 27
Sociability 11
Sounds and communication 41
Southern river terrapins 59, **59**
Spawning 6
Spectacled leaf monkeys 45, **45**
Speed 33, 43
Spiders 49
Spider wasps **57**
Spotted eagle rays 26-27, **26-27**
Spotted owls 8-9, **8-9**
Spraying 46-47
Squirrels **25**
Steppe eagles 48
Strength and muscles 21
Striped skunks 46-47, **46-47**
Sugar gliders 24, 36, **36**
Swimming 12-13, 26-27, 50, 58, 70

T

Tabby cats **24**
Tadpoles 30, **30**, 34, **34**, 38, **38, 49**, 50, **50**
Tails 14-15, 26, 41, 46, 50, 55, 62, 66-67
Talons 9
Tarantulas 45, **45**
Teeth 15, 52
Texas horned lizards **59**
Three-striped poison frogs 30, **30**
Tiger salamanders 73, **73**
Timber wolves 69, **69**
Toucans 73, **73**
Trees 10-11, 14-15, 61-62
Turtles 13, **13, 24**, 49, **49**
Tymbals 41

V

Veterinarians 22, 64
Virginia opossums 36, **36,** 66-67, **66-67**

W

Walking 12-15, 19-20, 50-51, 74
Warthogs 59, **59**
Wasps 10
Weaver birds 11, **11**
Weddell seals 35, **35**
Weight. *See* size and weight
Whales **56**, 72, **72-73**
Whiskers 71
Wings 8, 40-41
Wrestling 52-53

Z

Zebras 73, **73**

Photo credits

Key: DT - Dreamstime.com; IS - iStock.com; SS - Shutterstock; GY - Getty

BG - Background; CL - Clockwise from top left; TtB - Top to bottom

Front Cover TtB: ©Mdorottya/DT, ©Eric Isselee/IS, ©PCHT/SS

Back Cover: ©Miroslav Hlavko/SS

Front Endpaper: ©Svehlik21/DT

Back Endpaper: ©Lynn Bystrom/DT

p. 1: ©Howard Nevitt, Jr./DT; pp. 2-3: ©Kerstin Waurick/IS/GY; pp. 4-5: ©1001slide/IS; pp. 6-7 BG: ©Secret Sea Visions/GY, CL: ©Jean-Philippe Varin/Science Source, ©Cathy Keifer/SS, ©imv/IS, ©ABDESIGN/IS, ©Luke Wein/SS, ©Stevenrussellsmithphotos/DT; pp. 8-9 TtB: ©Nick Dale/GY, ©kajornyot/IS; pp. 10-11 BG: ©Brendon Cremer/NIS/GY, CL: ©Pavel Krasensky/SS, ©EcoPrint/SS, ©&#169 Andre Maritz/IS, ©wundervisuals/IS, ©National Park Service; pp. 12-13: ©FrankvandenBergh/IS, CL: ©Vishnevskiy Vasily/SS, ©Frank Leung/IS, ©Heidi & Hans-Juergen Koch/GY, ©Frank Leung/IS; pp. 14-15 BG: ©David & Micha Sheldon/F1 ONLINE/Superstock, p. 14 TtB: ©Hung_Chung-Chih/IS, ©Dr. Axel Gebauer/naturepl.com; pp. 16-17: ©Tony Campbell/SS; pp. 18-19 BG: ©Andries Alberts/SS, CL: ©Victor Tyakht/SS, ©TK, ©Ricochet69/DT; pp. 20-21 BG: ©Rita Kochmarjova/SS, p. 20: ©Rita Kochmarjova/SS, p. 21: ©Roberto A Sanchez/IS; pp. 22-23 BG: ©Silkenphotography/DT, Game board: ©Jenkedco/DT, ©Anna Yakimova/DT, ©Andy Katz/DT, ©Anna Yakimova/DT, ©Bigandt/DT, ©Caroline Henri/DT, ©Susan Chiang/IS, ©Laindiapiaroa/DT, ©wavebreakmedia/SS, ©Pressmaster/SS, ©Christopher Futcher/IS, ©bikeriderlondon/SS, p. 22: ©Alexander Raths/DT, ©SpeedKingz/SS; pp. 24-25 BG: ©Rouzes/IS, 1st row LtR: ©Helen Sushitskaya/

SS, ©Max Topchii/SS, ©Dmitry Naumov/DT, ©Stangot/DT, ©Saman527/DT, 2nd row LtR: ©Rita Kochmarjova/SS, ©National Park Service, 3rd row LtR: ©Benjamin Simeneta/DT, ©Eugene Sergeev/SS, ©USFWS, ©hasrullnizam/SS, ©boykung/SS; pp. 26-27 BG: ©Whitcomberd/DT, p. 26: ©Matt_Potenski/IS, p. 27: ©gremlin/IS; pp. 28-29: ©FabioMaffei/IS; pp. 30-31 BG: ©KatePhotographer/GY, CL: ©Orhan Cam/SS, ©danefromspain/IS, ©wavebreakmedia/SS, ©Ryan M. Bolton/SS; pp. 32-33 BG: ©maten/GY, p. 32: ©KAdams66/IS, p. 33: ©Algirdas Gelazius/DT; pp. 34-35 BG: ©Norbert Wu/Minden Pictures/GY, CL: ©Dr Morley Read/SS, ©Noah Kahn/USFWS, ©Vladislav T. Jirousek/SS; pp. 36-37: ©THPStock/Purestock, p. 36 TtB: ©Gary Meszaros/GY, ©Roland Seitre/Minden Picutres/GY, ©Pete Oxford/GY; pp. 38-39 BG: ©Johnny Johnson/GY; CL: ©EcoPrint/SS, ©Design Pics via AP, ©Tomisickova Tatyana/SS, ©Annie Katz/GY; pp. 40-41 BG: ©Dennis Van De Water/DT, p. 40: ©Zhitao Li/DT, p. 41: ©zaidi razak/SS; pp. 42-43: ©Justas Jaruševičius/DT; pp. 44-45 BG: ©Katarina Christenson/SS, p. 45 TtB: ©Barcroft/Contributor/GY, ©clearviewstock/SS, ©Hyde Peranitti/SS, ©National Park Service, ©Borirak Mongkolget/DT; pp. 46-47: ©Kenneth Canning/IS, p. 46: ©Betty4240/IS, p. 47: ©Bildagentur Zoonar GmbH/SS; pp. 48-49 BG: ©Rouzes/IS, 1st row LtR: ©Dracozlat/DT, ©Peter Van Der Zwaag/DT, ©Jeff Foot/Discovery Communications, LLC, ©Anneka/SS, ©Frank Luerweg/IS, 2nd row LtR: ©Alejandro Rivera/IS, ©mattwicks/IS, 3rd row LtR: ©timsimages/SS, ©BSIP/Contributor/GY, ©Mark Kostich/IS, ©Napat_Polchoke/IS, ©Henrik_L/IS; pp. 50-51 CL: ©Maurizio Bonora/IS, ©Andrew Dernie/GY, ©Eric Isselee/SS, ©Kamil Macniak/SS, ©Gerard Lacz/age fotostock/Superstock, ©Anankkml/DT; pp. 52-53 BG: ©rpbirdman/IS, CL: ©Debbie Steinhausser/SS, ©Paul Banton/DT, ©Jonathan Cohen/IS, ©Aughty Venable/DT; pp. 54-55 BG: ©Alona Rjabceva/IS; p. 54 LtR: ©Skyhobo/IS, ©Horhes/IS; pp. 56-57 BG: ©Rouzes/IS,

1st row LtR: ©Fieldwork/DT, ©Lmspencer/SS, ©Nate Allred/SS, ©Viacheslav Belyaev/DT, ©Ethan Daniels/SS, 2nd row LtR: ©Neil_Burton/IS, ©EcoPrint/SS, 3rd row LtR: ©Scay21/DT, ©Andries Alberts/DT, ©Kletr/SS, ©Aumsama/SS; pp. 58-59 BG: ©Fahkamram/SS, p. 58 CL: ©Steve Meese/SS, ©U.S. Fish and Wildlife Service, ©Eric Gevaert/SS, ©Kristina Vackova/SS, ©Andrea Willmore/SS, ©Don Fink/SS, p. 59 CL: ©Mikael Males/DT, ©Matt Jeppson/SS, ©U.S. Fish and Wildlife Service, ©Alberto Loyo/SS, ©David Rasmus/SS, ©NPS/Diane Renkin, ©Vladimir Wrangel/SS, ©Wrangel/DT, ©Michael Sheehan/DT; pp. 60-61 BG: ©Wellesenterprises/DT, CL: ©Debbie Steinhausser/SS, ©Helen Birkin/SS, ©Angela Waye/SS, ©Wolfgang Bayer/Discovery Communications, LLC; pp. 62-63 BG: ©alisontoonphotographer/IS, p. 62: ©FRANKHILDEBRAND/IS, p. 63: ©Jason Ondreicka/DT; pp. 64-65 BG: ©TK, Game board: ©Ryan Moehring/USFWS, ©Kimberly Tamkun/USFWS, ©Kimberly Tamkun/USFWS, ©Kimberly Tamkun/USFWS, ©Kimberly Fraser/USFWS, ©Kimberly Tamkun/USFWS, ©Jared Martin/USFWS, ©Stewart Brand/USFWS, ©Ben Novak/USFWS, ©Steve Segin/USFWS, ©Kimberly Fraser/USFWS, ©NPS, ©Ryan Moehring/USFWS; pp. 66-67: ©stanley45/IS; pp. 68-69 Top: ©cullenphotos/IS, CL: ©Volodymyr Burdiak/SS, ©Guenter Guni/IS, ©Peter Leahy/SS, ©Diane Picard/SS, ©1001slide/IS, ©Karoline Cullen/DT; pp. 70-71 BG: ©Chase Dekker/DT, p. 70: ©worldswildlifewonders/SS, p. 71: ©Fred Goldstein/DT; pp. 72-73 CL: ©Harold Stiver/DT, ©MattiaATH/SS, ©tamers1/IS, ©Vladimir Melnik/DT, ©Serena Livingston/DT, ©K. Kristina Drake/USGS; pp. 74-79 BG: ©MadamLead/IS/GY; , p. 74 What's my name TtB: ©Alis Leonte/SS, ©Geoffrey Kuchera/SS, ©Geoffrey Kuchera/SS, ©Yulia_B/SS, ©Best dog photo/SS, Baby steps TtB: ©Rita Kochmarjova/SS, ©Dan Clark/USFWS, ©vladsilver/SS, ©Aneese/IS; pp. 76-77: 1st column TtB: ©Chase Dekker/DT, ©Tjkphotography/DT, 2nd column: ©NOAA, 3rd column: ©LAByrne/IS/GY, 4th column: ©DT

ANIMAL BITES

baby animals

SCOUT BOOKS • MEDIA

Produced by Scout Books & Media Inc
President and Project Director Susan Knopf
Writer Dorothea DePrisco
Editor Ellen Stamper
Project Manager Brittany Gialanella
Copyeditor Beth Adelman
Proofreader Michael Centore
Indexer Andrea Baron
Designer Dirk Kaufman
Prepress by Andrij Borys Associates, LLC

Advisor Michael Rentz, PhD
Lecturer in Mammalogy, Iowa State University

Special thanks to the Time Inc. Books team: Margot Schupf, Anja Schmidt, Beth Sutinis, Deirdre Langeland, Georgia Morrissey, Megan Pearlman, Melodie George, and Sue Chodakiewicz.

Special thanks to the Discovery and Animal Planet creative and licensing team: Denny Chen, Tracy Conner, Elizabeta Ealy, Robert Marick, Doris Miller, Sue Perez-Jackson, and Janet Tsuei.

© 2017 Discovery Communications, LLC.

ANIMAL PLANET™ and the logos are trademarks of Discovery Communications, LLC, used under license. All rights reserved.
animalplanet.com

LIBERTY STREET

Published by Liberty Street, an imprint of Time Inc. Books
225 Liberty Street
New York, New York 10281

LIBERTY STREET is a trademark of Time Inc.

All rights reserved. No part of this book may be reproduced in any form or by any electronic or mechanical means, including information storage and retrieval systems, without permission in writing from the publisher, except by a reviewer, who may quote brief passages in a review.

ISBN 10: 1-61893-178-4
ISBN 13: 978-1-61893-178-8

First edition, 2017

Printed and bound in China

1 TLF 17

Time Inc. Books products may be purchased for business or promotional use. For information on bulk purchases, please contact Christi Crowley in the Special Sales Department at (845) 895-9858.

To order Time Inc. Books Collector's Editions, please call (800) 327-6388, Monday through Friday, 7 a.m.-9 p.m., Central Time.

We welcome your comments and suggestions about Time Inc. Books.
Please write to us at:
Time Inc. Books

Attention: Book Editors

P.O. Box 62310
Tampa, Florida 33662-2310